Learning About
Books & Libraries

2

Carol K. Lee & Janet Langford

UpstartBooks

Fort Atkinson, Wisconsin

Additional Books by Carol K. Lee

Learning About Books & Libraries: A Gold Mine of Games
Carol Lee and Janet Langford (1-57950-051-X)

Storytime Companion: Learning Games & Activities for Schools & Libraries Carol Lee and Janet Langford (1-57950-019-6)

57 Games to Play in the Library or Classroom
Carol Lee and Fay Edwards (1-57950-014-5)

Published by UpstartBooks
W5527 Highway 106
P.O. Box 800
Fort Atkinson, Wisconsin 53538-0800
1-800-448-4887

Contents

Introduction

Learning About Books & Libraries 2 supplements *Learning About Books & Libraries: A Gold Mine of Games* and *57 Games to Play in the Library or Classroom*. Along with *Storytime Companion*, these books provide a wealth of ideas to enliven teaching about the media center and its resources. The format of this book follows the popular format of *Learning About Books & Libraries* and *57 Games to Play in the Library or Classroom*. Grade-level recommendations are at the top of each game description and in the index. Most of the games may be played with at least three grade levels, depending on the difficulty of the questions, the skill taught or the literature-based books that relate to the games.

Making and Playing the Games

Examples of the game boards, patterns and sample questions are included to expedite the preparation of the games. Also included are estimates for the preparation time if you use the patterns and questions provided. Most of the games do not take more than 30 minutes to make. This edition contains more copy-ready pages, more games that can be made in less than 30 minutes and more games that can be used on the primary level.

Learning About Books & Libraries 2 includes suggested questions and answers as well as book lists for certain themes. These minimize the preparation time involved for the teacher or media specialist. You may use the suggested questions or you may devise your own questions that are specific to your lessons.

Many of the games can be drawn on the chalkboard, but directions for making a permanent game board are also included because it is our experience that most teachers prefer to create something they can use again and again.

When making or selecting game markers, it's important to choose items that the entire class can easily see. We suggest clips, clamps or clothespins because these are easy to move around the edges of the board. They may be purchased from a grocery store, hardware store or a discount store. You can use Post-It notepaper or double-stick tape with game pieces to mark the moves that are away from the edges of the game board. The notepaper or tape will need to be replaced after each game.

Many of the games are intended for students to work in groups. We feel that working in teams and dividing the researching and recording responsibilities are effective approaches to learning. Some games may require students to do preliminary research with their teams. The directions suggest when a game is best played with teams or when preliminary research is required.

The average time for playing the games should not be more than 30 minutes. A short review of the particular skill the game covers, a brief introduction to the game and the rules should precede each game.

How to Use This Book

The games are intended as a follow up to lessons on certain skills, not to introduce or teach these skills. They are designed to enhance the lessons, review the lessons or serve as an activity following a particular story.

Each game has suggested grade levels for effective use, simple statements of purpose and directions to make and play the games. The directions also include the approximate time needed to make the game and the items needed to play the game, such as a timer, spinner or markers.

The first group of games relates to resources of the media center. These games review books and genres, terms related to the media center and resources of the media center. A biography game at the end of the chapter reviews the biography section. An introduction to this section is usually made to students at about the second-grade level and continues through fourth grade.

The second group has two games that review call numbers and the third group of games relates to fiction books. The fiction games review plots, characters, settings, authors and Newbery and Caldecott Medal winners. We have selected only fiction titles that are currently in print. Similar books not in print may still be in your library and you may adapt the games to fit these books. We have suggested books that we feel are likely to be found in most school library collections.

The last section includes an assortment of games that can be used with thematic units or to follow up a particular book. While we have suggested specific book titles, we may have excluded books that work as well as or better than the ones we've chosen.

We have made an effort not to reuse certain games; rather, we have tried to provide a variety of games that can be used as is or easily adapted to use with other skills.

At the end of the book is a grade appropriate skills index, a feature that is continued from *Learning About Books & Libraries: A Gold Mine of Games*. These two indexes, plus the game finder index in *57 Games to Play in the Library or Classroom*, will help you easily locate relevant games when planning your lesson.

Chatter Books

Purpose

To have students discuss books.

To Make

Copy the activity sheet on page 8, one for each student.

⏰ Preparation time—10 minutes

To Play

Give each student a copy of the activity sheet. Direct the students to ask each other the questions that are on the sheet. If a student answers "yes," their name should be written in the appropriate block. There should only be one name per block and all nine blocks should have a different name. A student's name should only appear once and the students should not share their answers with each other.

Set a 15-minute time limit for the students to "chat" with each other. Then recognize the students who completed all nine questions. Review the appropriate answers with the class.

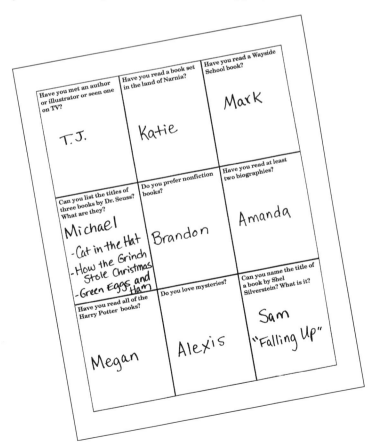

Chatter Books—Activity Sheet

Have you met an author or illustrator or seen one on TV?	Have you read a book set in the land of Narnia?	Have you read a Wayside School book?
Can you list the titles of three books by Dr. Seuss? What are they?	Do you prefer nonfiction books?	Have you read at least two biographies?
Have you read all of the Harry Potter books?	Do you love mysteries?	Can you name the title of a book by Shel Silverstein? What is it?

Word Play

Purpose

To review terms related to the resources of the media center.

To Make

Copy the chart on page 10 onto card stock. Cut the cards out and laminate them for repeated use. Shuffle and stack the cards.

You will need a timer for this activity.

⏰ Preparation time—15 minutes

To Play

Divide the class into two to four teams. Tell the students that they have 30 seconds per turn. The object of the game is to get as many points as possible in the allotted time.

Direct one team to start the game by taking a card from the stack and giving his or her team members a clue related to the word on the card (e.g., the clue for the fiction card might be *The Trumpet of the Swan*). When the team members say the word on the card, another card may be turned over. Each team is allowed to throw out one card per turn if they cannot guess the word.

When the 30 seconds are up, the team's score is the number of correct responses.

Continue with the next team. Have the teams take turns through several rounds, but do not repeat any of the clues. If you play more than one round, change the order so that the team that began the first round goes last and the last goes first.

The team with the most points wins the game.

Fiction	Novel
Software	Reference
Picture Book	Atlas
Biography	Author
Call Number	Story Collection
Illustrator	CD–ROM
Nonfiction	Caldecott Winner
Unabridged Dictionary	Almanac
Newbery Winner	Autobiography

4 X 4

Purpose

To review general information related to the resources of the media center.

To Make

Draw the game board below on the chalkboard or dry-erase board.

Copy and cut out the numbers from page 13.

Use different colors of chalk or markers to mark the X's and O's.

⏰ Preparation time—15 minutes

To Play

Put the numbers in a paper bag. Divide the class into two teams, the X's and the O's. Ask the member of one team a question (see the sample questions on page 12). If the player gives the correct answer, he or she pulls a number out of the bag and puts the team's marker on the appropriate number on the game board. Follow the same procedure with the other team.

The object of the game is to get four X's or O's in a row. You may vary the game so the object is to win by having the numbers on the four corners (e.g., 1, 4, 13, 16) or by having any four numbers form a block (i.e., 1, 2, 5, 6 or 3, 4, 7, 8).

If an "Erase one mark from the other team" card appears, change a mark on the board. When a team wins, erase the marks on the board, put all the cards back in the bag and start a new game.

1	2	3	4
5	6	7	8
9	10	11	12
13	14	15	16

sample game board

Sample Questions for 4 x 4

1. Where is the title page found in a book? *(front part of a book)*

2. Name two pieces of information other than the title found on the title page. *(author, illustrator, publisher)*

3. What is the difference between what an author does and what an illustrator does? *(an author writes the books; an illustrator draws the pictures)*

4. What does a publisher do for a book? *(prints books, sells books)*

5. Is the name of the publisher usually found on the top or bottom of the title page? *(bottom)*

6. What does copyright mean? *(the item is legally protected against illegal copying)*

7. What is the symbol for copyright? *(a circle with a "c" inside)*

8. Is the copyright date always on the title page? *(no)*

9. What page sometimes follows the title page? *(table of contents, foreword)*

10. What information is found on the contents page? *(book chapters, page numbers)*

11. The items on the contents page are usually arranged: *(c)*
    a. alphabetically by stories
    b. alphabetically by authors' names
    c. sequentially by page numbers

12. Do all books have a contents page? *(no)*

13. What is a glossary? *(a short dictionary at the end of a book)*

14. Where is the index found? *(at the end of a book)*

15. Do all books have either an index or a glossary? *(no)*

16. Sometimes there is a bibliography at the end of a book. What is a bibliography? *(a list of books on a topic)*

17. What part of a book has words in alphabetical order and gives page numbers for finding information? *(an index)*

18. Where can you find information about all the resources in the media center? *(in an online catalog)*

19. Besides the title of a book, what other information is found on the spine of a book? *(the call number)*

20. Describe a nonfiction call number. *(numbers with 3 letters from author's last name)*

21. Explain this call number: B FRA. *(B for biography; FRA for the last name of the person the book is about—Benjamin Franklin)*

22. Do the three letters of a fiction call number come from the title or author's name? *(author's last name)*

23. How are nonfiction books arranged on the shelves? *(by Dewey numbers)*

24. How are biography books arranged on the shelves? *(by the last name of the person the book is about)*

25. How are fiction books arranged? *(by author's last name)*

26. Are all fiction books shelved in the same section? *(no, easy fiction books are separated from longer fiction books)*

1	2	3
4	5	6
7	8	9
10	11	12
13	14	15
16	Erase one mark from the other team.	Erase one mark from the other team.

Lucky Numbers

Purpose

To review various genres of books.

To Make

Copy pages 15 and 16 onto card stock. Cut the cards out. Put the Lucky Number cards into one paper bag. Put the other cards in another paper bag.

⏰ Preparation time—15 minutes

To Play

Divide the class into two teams. Have each team select a person to pull the cards out of the bag. Take three cards out of the Lucky Number bag. Tell the class what they are. These are the Lucky Numbers for the first game.

Have the designated person from one team pull out a card and read it. The team calls out an answer. If the answer is correct, the card remains with the team. If the answer is incorrect, the card is put back at the bottom of the stack. Have the teams take turns.

For example:

Animal Character—Clifford, the big red dog

Dr. Seuss Character—Grinch

The object of the game is to collect cards with the three Lucky Numbers on them. If a team gets an Any Number card, they can use it as one of the Lucky Numbers.

The first team to get all three Lucky Numbers, wins. Continue with another game if time permits.

1 Title of a fable	**2** Title of a folktale	**3** Animal character
4 Title of a mystery	**5** Subject of a book in the 500 (Science) section	**6** Subject of a biography
7 Subject of a book in the 400 (Language) section	**8** Female character	**9** Subject of a book in the 600 (Applied Science) section
10 Character in a Dr. Seuss book	**1** Male character	**2** Subject of a book in the 700 (Art, Music, Sports) section
3 Subject of a book in the 900 (Geography, Travel, History) section	**4** Title of a fiction book	**5** Title of an adventure book
6 Title of a Caldecott Award winner	**7** Title of a picture book	**8** Title of a reference book
9 Title of a Newbery Award winner	**10** Name of a folk hero	Any number
Any number	Any number	Take a number from the other team.

Lucky Numbers—Lucky Number Cards

Lucky Number 1	Lucky Number 2	Lucky Number 3
Lucky Number 4	Lucky Number 5	Lucky Number 6
Lucky Number 7	Lucky Number 8	Lucky Number 9
Lucky Number 10		

Circle Book Toss

Purpose

To review information about books.

To Make

Make two copies of pages 18–19 for grades two and three. Make four copies of page 18 for grade one. There should be a total of 12 circles. Do not cut out the circles.

Arrange the pages in a large square on the floor (the sides of the pages should be touching). Tape the pages together. Use masking tape to tape a line about 1½ to 2 feet from the square. The line is where the students will stand to pitch the cap. Test the length with a student before class.

You will need a milk jug cap for the students to toss.

Each student will need a book.

⏰ Preparation time—15 minutes

To Play

Divide the class into two teams.

Have the teams take turns tossing their caps into the square. When a student successfully pitches the cap partially or completely into one of the circles, he or she should give the appropriate information from his or her book.

If part of the cap lands on two circles, the student may decide which circle he or she will answer.

Scoring:

1. No point for the wrong answer.

2. One point for the correct answer if the cap is partially in a circle.

3. Two points for the correct answer if the cap is partially in a circle and it is top side up.

4. Three points for the correct answer if the cap is completely in the circle and touches no lines.

5. Four points for the correct answer if the cap is completely in the circle, touches no lines and is top side up.

After each player has had a turn, or an even number of turns, the team with the most points wins the game.

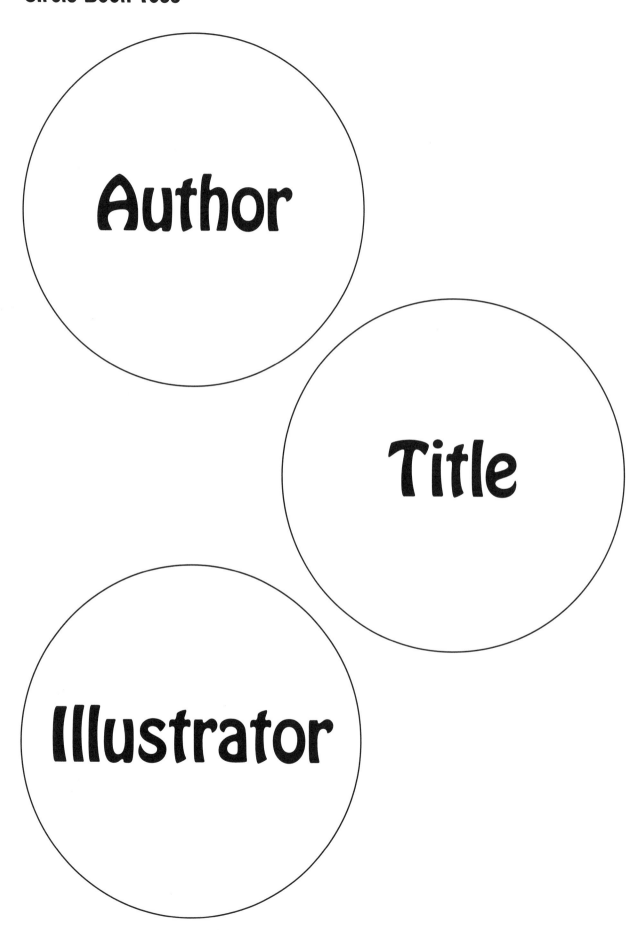

Author

Title

Illustrator

Publisher

Copyright
Date

Call
Number

Biography Brainstorm

Purpose

To review the biography section.

To Make

Reproduce the game board below on poster board. Put six or seven stars randomly next to T's and F's.

Copy the bonus cards on page 22 onto card stock and cut them out. Shuffle the cards and put them in a stack, face down.

You will need clothespins or large clips to mark the moves around the board. Use a different color for each team.

⏰ Preparation time—30 minutes

To Play

Divide the class into two teams. Read a biography statement to a player from one team. Use the sample statements from page 21 or make up your own. The player should respond true or false.

If the response is correct, move the team marker to the closest T or F that corresponds with the answer. If the answer is incorrect, do not move the team's marker. The starred letters indicate bonus moves. If a player lands on one, he or she should turn over a bonus card and move according to the directions.

Have the teams take turns. The first team to reach the finish wins the game.

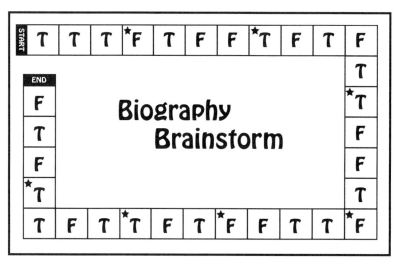

sample game board

Sample True and False Statements for Biography Brainstorm

1. A biography is a book about the life of a real person. *(T)*

2. The biography books are shelved next to the picture books in the media center. *(F)*

3. The biography books are arranged on the shelf alphabetically by the author's last name. *(F)*

4. All biography books have the letter A on the spine. *(F)*

5. Collective biography books have the numbers 920 on the spine. *(T)*

6. An autobiography is when a person writes about someone else. *(F)*

7. The call number for an autobiography is the same as an individual biography. *(T)*

8. A book about Paul Bunyan is a biography. *(F)*

9. The call number for a biography about Martin Luther King Jr. is **B Kin.** *(T)*

10. A book about the life of Helen Keller would be at the end of the biography section. *(F)*

11. A book about George Washington Carver would be found after a book about George Washington. *(F)*

12. The call number for the book *Minty: A Story of Young Harriet Tubman* by Alan Schroeder would be **B Sch**. *(F)*

13. Stuart Little is not a biography. *(T)*

14. Thomas Edison might be the subject of a biography about an inventor. *(T)*

15. Rosa Parks might be the subject of a biography about an explorer. *(F)*

16. A book about the life cycle of a butterfly is a biography. *(F)*

17. A biography call number consists of letters and a nonfiction call number consists of numbers. *(T)*

18. A fiction call number and a biography call number are the same. *(F)*

19. Books about folk heroes such as Robin Hood and John Henry are not biographies. *(T)*

Biography Brainstorm—Bonus Cards

Go to the next letter.	Go to the next letter.	Go to the next letter.	Go two spaces ahead.	Take a flying leap! Move four spaces!
Go to the next letter.	Go to the next "T."	Go to the next "F."	Go two spaces ahead.	Take a flying leap! Move four spaces!
Go to the next letter.	Go to the next "T."	Go to the next "F."	Go two spaces ahead.	Go three spaces ahead.
Go to the next letter.	Go to the next "T."	Go to the next "F."	Go two spaces ahead.	Go three spaces ahead.
Go to the next letter.	Go to the next "T."	Go to the next "F."	Go two spaces ahead.	Go three spaces ahead.

Small Steps, Giant Steps

Purpose

To review call numbers.

To Make

Copy one game sheet from page 24 for each student.

Copy the step cards from page 25 onto card stock and cut them out. Put the cards in a paper bag.

Use masking tape to mark the start and finish lines for the game.

⏰ Preparation time—20 minutes

To Play

Divide the class into two teams. Give each student a game sheet. Have each team select a runner. The object of the game is to have the team's runner be the first to cross the finish line. Show where to start and finish the race.

Direct the two runners to stand at the starting line. A team member from one team selects a call number (not necessarily in the order it appears on the page) and the item from the other column that best matches it.

If the answer is correct, the student can draw a step card from the bag. The team runner takes the number of steps stated on the card. If the answer is incorrect, no step card is drawn. Answers to the game sheet are provided below.

The first team to reach the finish line wins.

Note: A "small step" is a step right in front (touching) of the other foot. A "giant step" is the longest stride possible (not a leap).

Answers: 1=10; 2=14; 3 =20; 4=22; 5=1; 6=9; 7=13; 8=16; 9=23; 10=18; 11=5; 12=19; 13=21; 14=3; 15=2; 16=6; 17=12; 18=7; 19=24; 20=8; 21=4; 22=15; 23=11; 24=17

Small Steps, Giant Steps—Match the Call Numbers

1. B Poc		1. story collection call number
2. 741.5		2. *Tales of a Fourth Grade Nothing* call number
3. 811 Sil		3. call number for a book about Jupiter
4. 292		4. *Dear Mr. Henshaw* call number
5. SC		5. folktale call number
6. E Wie		6. call number for a book on Abraham Lincoln
7. REF 031		7. call number for *Charlotte's Web* or *Stuart Little*
8. F Lew		8. call number for a book about Mexico
9. VR		9. call number for *Tuesday* or another book by David Wiesner
10. F Pau		10. call number for a biography about Pocahontas
11. 398.2		11. call number for a Harry Potter book
12. E Seu		12. call number for a French dictionary
13. 796.8		13. call number for an encyclopedia
14. 523.45		14. call number for a "how-to-draw" book
15. F Blu		15. call number for a book about Helen Keller
16. B Lin		16. call number for a book set in Narnia
17. 443.21		17. call number for a biography about Harriet Tubman
18. F Whi		18. call number for *Canyons* by Gary Paulsen
19. 567.9		19. call number for *How the Grinch Stole Christmas*
20. 972		20. call number for a Shel Silverstein poetry book
21. F Cle		21. call number for a karate book
22. B Kel		22. call number for Greek myths
23. F Row		23. call number for a video recording
24. B Tub		24. call number for books on dinosaurs

1 Giant Step	2 Giant Steps	3 Giant Steps
1 Giant Step	2 Giant Steps	3 Giant Steps
5 Small Steps	6 Small Steps	7 Small Steps
5 Small Steps	6 Small Steps	7 Small Steps
1 Small Step Back	1 Small Step Back	2 Small Steps Back
2 Giant Steps	1 Giant Step	4 Giant Steps

Find That Book!

Purpose

To review locating a nonfiction book.

To Make

Copy one game sheet from page 27 for each student.

You will need a timer for this game and each student will need a pencil.

⏰ Preparation time—5 minutes

To Play

Divide the class into four teams. Give a game sheet to each student.

The object of the game is to locate the titles of the books for the call numbers listed. Only one team goes to the shelves at a time. Each team has five minutes at the shelves. The teams should divide the task so that everyone is not hunting for the same book.

On "Go," the team races to the shelves to locate the titles. Players may help their team members.

At "Stop," the team members must return to their seats. Continue until each team has had a turn. Then go over the answers. The team with the most correct answers wins the game.

Find That Book!

Write a title of a book for each call number listed below.

398.2 _____

641.5 _____

599 _____

811 _____

292 _____

460 _____

796.3 _____

551.6 _____

917 _____

793.7 _____

333 _____

629.4 _____

Cover Four

Purpose

To review elements related to fiction books.

To Make

Copy pages 30–31 onto card stock. Cut the cards out, shuffle them and put them in a stack.

Copy one score sheet from page 29 for each team.

You will need eight beans, buttons or small squares of card stock to use for markers.

⏰ Preparation time—20 minutes

To Play

Divide the class into two teams. Each team selects a scorekeeper. Give the scorekeepers the score sheets and the markers.

Direct one team member to take a card from the stack. The player identifies the information on the card as character, plot, setting or title page information. If the answer is correct, the team's scorekeeper places the marker on the block that relates to the answer.

Have the teams take turns. The first team to cover four blocks to form a square wins the game.

Title	Call Number	Character	Plot
Author	Illustrator	Title	Setting
Plot	Character	Setting	Illustrator
Call Number	Author	Plot	Character

Cover Four—Cards

Harry and the Terrible Whatzit	Story and pictures by Paul Brett Johnson	by Dav Pilkey	*It Looked Like Spilt Milk*
Strega Nona's house, in Calabria	a little white dog nobody wanted	Madeline's house in Paris	*Tops and Bottoms*
Abe Lincoln's Hat	the North Pole where Lars, the little polar bear, lives	Written and illustrated by Eileen Christelow	A housekeeper does everything wrong on her first day on the job.
Students welcome their teacher back after a "witch" of a substitute teacher.	Verdi's home—a small tropical island	Arthur wants to lose his "baby" teeth to escape Francine's teasing.	Room 207 where Miss Viola Swamp is the substitute teacher.

The Kissing Hand	Written and illustrated by Hans de Beer	East 88th Street, where Lyle, Lyle Crocodile lives	The city grows around a little house, making her unhappy.
a mouse who is given a cookie	the animals who crawl into a mitten to escape the cold winter day	the deep, blue sea, where the Rainbow Fish lives	Alexander's day went from bad to a terrible, horrible, no good, very bad day.
A week of eating fruits and snacks ends with the caterpillar settling into a cocoon.	the biggest, reddest dog on Emily Elizabeth's street	a turtle named Franklin	George and Martha, two hippopotamus friends
toy bear who is missing a button on his overalls	E Seu	letters of the alphabet climb up a coconut tree	E Bri

Listen Carefully!

Purpose

To encourage students to listen carefully to a story.

To Make

Select a fiction book or a folktale to read to the students.

⏰ Preparation time—10 minutes

To Play

Divide the class into two teams. Have each team designate a spokesperson.

Read the selected text (a few chapters) for about 20 minutes. Have the students write questions about the story, then give them to their spokesperson. No additional questions may be handed to the spokesperson once the game has begun.

Designate an amount of time for questions. Direct the spokesperson to select one question to ask per turn. The other team decides on a correct response and has its spokesperson give the answer. A team may not ask a question if it does not know the correct answer.

If the answer is correct, that team gets to ask a question. If the answer is incorrect, the team that asked the question gets a point. The game continues with the teams taking turns asking and answering questions.

When one team runs out of questions, the other team receives bonus points for every question it asks before the designated time is up. The team with the most points earned (incorrect answers from the other team and bonus points at the end of the game) wins the game.

Note: *Encourage students to think of questions related to the words used in the text (e.g., verbs, adjectives, etc.) as well as questions related to the characters, plot and setting.*

Wipeout!

Purpose

To acquaint students with well-known authors and the books they have written.

To Make

Print the titles of the books listed on page 34 on 3" x 5" index cards, one title per card.
On the chalkboard write:

Team A	Team B	Team C
WIPEOUT	WIPEOUT	WIPEOUT

Also write these authors on the chalkboard:

1. Eric Carle

2. Don Freeman

3. Ezra Jack Keats

4. Leo Lionni

5. Dr. Seuss

⏰ Approximate time to introduce authors—2 to 3 weeks

⏰ Preparation time—30 minutes

To Play

Acquaint the students with the authors listed above by reading their books.

Stack the index cards face down. Read aloud, then have the children read aloud with you, the names of the authors listed on the chalkboard. Explain that the students must decide which author wrote the book on the index card that they draw.

Divide the class into three teams: A, B and C. Ask a member from Team A to draw a card. Read the book title on the card aloud. Team A has 30 seconds to decide the author of that book. If Team A answers correctly, a member from that team comes to the board and erases, or wipes out, one letter from their "WIPEOUT." The other teams follow the same procedure. The team that wipes out the most, or all, of their letters wins.

Sample Books to Use

Eric Carle

The Grouchy Ladybug. Harper Collins, 1999.

The Very Busy Spider. Philomel Books, 1984.

The Very Hungry Caterpillar. Philomel Books, 1987.

The Very Lonely Firefly. Penguin Putnam, 1999.

The Very Quiet Cricket. Philomel Books, 1990.

Don Freeman

Corduroy. Puffin Books, 1977.

Dandelion. Viking, 1964.

Guard Mouse. Viking, 1967.

Mop Top. Puffin Books, 1978.

A Pocket for Corduroy. Penguin Books, 1980.

Ezra Jack Keats

Goggles! Puffin Books, 1998.

A Letter to Amy. Viking, 1998.

Peter's Chair. Viking, 1998.

The Snowy Day. Puffin Books, 1978.

Whistle for Willie. Viking, 1998.

Leo Lionni

Alexander and the Wind-Up Mouse. Knopf/Pantheon, 1974.

Fish Is Fish. Pantheon, 1970.

Frederick. Random House, 1973.

Inch by Inch. Scholastic, 1994.

Swimmy. Scholastic, 1989.

Dr. Seuss

The Cat in the Hat. Random House, 1997.

Green Eggs and Ham. Random House, 1976.

Horton Hatches the Egg. Random House, 1976.

How the Grinch Stole Christmas. Random House, 1976.

One Fish, Two Fish, Red Fish, Blue Fish. Random House Beginner Books, 1976

Tic Tac Toe

Purpose

To review familiar picture books.

To Make

Draw a large Tic Tac Toe grid onto 8½" x 11" card stock. Laminate.

Make nine copies each of the bear and the fish on page 37. Color, laminate and cut out. These are the markers.

Cut nine 1-inch pieces of self-adhesive Velcro strips and pull each piece apart. Stick one side of each piece to each grid on the Tic Tac Toe board. Stick the matching pieces to the fish and bear markers.

⏰ Preparation time—45 minutes

To Play

Divide the class into two teams, the Bears and the Fish. Explain to the class that the object of the game is to have their markers be three in a row, either vertically, horizontally or diagonally.

Ask a Bear team member a question from the list on pages 36–37 or from questions that you create. If the Bear answers the question correctly, he or she places a Bear on the Tic Tac Toe grid. Continue with a player from the Fish team.

The first team to have Tic Tac Toe wins the game.

Books to Use

Use the book lists from Picture Detective on pages 38–39 and Pickin' Time on page 55.

Sample Questions for Tic Tac Toe

1. Which insect was grouchy?   *(ladybug)*

2. Name the insect that ate and ate until it turned itself into a beautiful butterfly. *(very hungry caterpillar)*

3. Which sea creature outgrew its home and had to find a new shell to live in? *(hermit crab)*

4. What kind of animal is Curious George?   *(monkey)*

5. What color is the hat that George's friend wears?   *(yellow)*

6. What is the name of the country where George was born?   *(Africa)*

7. Who is Clifford?   *(a dog)*

8. Who owns Clifford?   *(Emily Elizabeth)*

9. Name one way that Clifford is different from all other dogs.   *(he is red, big)*

10. Who went on an imaginary trip to where the wild things are?   *(Max)*

11. Which meal did Max get back in time to eat?   *(supper)*

12. What animal found a grain of wheat?   *(Little Red Hen)*

13. Why didn't the Little Red Hen share her bread with her friends?   *(they didn't help with the work)*

14. What pond animal floated through the air on lily pads?   *(frog)*

15. What little girl was almost eaten by a big, tricky wolf?   *(Little Red Riding Hood)*

16. Who was Little Red Riding Hood going to visit?   *(Granny)*

17. How many monkeys jumped on the bed?   *(five)*

18. What part of their bodies did the monkeys hurt when they fell off the bed? *(their heads)*

19. Who did mama monkey call when her babies fell off the bed?   *(doctor)*

20. What advice did the doctor give mama monkey when her babies bumped their heads? *(no more jumping on the bed)*

21. What did the first little pig use to build his house?   *(straw)*

22. What did the second little pig use to build his house?   *(twigs)*

23. What did the third little pig use to build his house?   *(bricks)*

24. Who huffed and puffed and blew the pig houses down?   *(the big bad wolf)*

25. When the big bad wolf came down the chimney, what was waiting for him? *(a kettle of boiling water)*

26. Which little animal was looking for a friend?   *(mouse)*

27. What did the three little kittens lose?   *(mittens)*

28. Who owns Willie?   *(Peter)*

29. What kind of animal is Willie?   *(a dog)*

30. Where did Snort drop baby bird?   *(tree, nest)*

31. Name one animal that baby bird asked, "Are you my mother?"   *(kitten, hen, dog, cow, Snort)*

32. Who was baby bird looking for?   *(mother)*

33. What fish learned to share?   *(Rainbow Fish)*

34. What wise sea animal gave good advice to the Rainbow Fish?   *(octopus)*

35. What did Rainbow Fish share with friends?   *(shiny scales)*

36. What did the cat in a Dr. Seuss book wear?   *(hat)*

37. Who came home right after the Cat in the Hat left?   *(mother)*

38. What kind of animal is Arthur?   *(aardvark)*

39. Why did Arthur try to run away from camp? *(he was scared)*

Make nine copies of each picture to use as the Tic Tac Toe markers.

Picture Detective

Purpose

To review familiar picture books.

To Make

Copy the detective cards from page 41 onto card stock. Laminate them, cut them out and place them in a paper bag.

Make four copies of the clue sheet on page 40. Laminate them.

⏰ Preparation time—20 minutes

To Play

Divide the class into four teams, and give each team a clue sheet. Ask a student from the first team to draw a detective card from the bag. Read the title on the card aloud. The first team looks at their clue sheet to find the picture that goes with that title. If the team makes a correct match, they keep their card. If they do not make a correct match, the card is returned to the bag.

Have the teams take turns. Repeat until all of the cards have been matched. The team that matches and collects the most cards wins the game.

Books to Use

Three Little Pigs by Aurelius Battaglia. Random House, 1977. A smart little pig outwits a hungry wolf.

Clifford the Big Red Dog by Norman Bridwell. Scholastic, 1985. A little red puppy grows into a very big red dog.

Arthur Goes to Camp by Marc Brown. Little, Brown, 1982. Strange happenings at camp make Arthur decide to run away.

Do You Want to Be My Friend? by Eric Carle. HarperCollins Children's Books, 1995. A little mouse searches for a friend.

The Very Hungry Caterpillar by Eric Carle. Philomel Books, 1987. A hungry caterpillar eats its way into becoming a beautiful butterfly.

Five Little Monkeys Jumping on the Bed by Eileen Christelow. Clarion Books, 1989. Five little monkeys fall off the bed and bump their heads.

Are You My Mother? by P. D. Eastman. Random House Books for Young Readers, 1998. A baby bird searches for its mother.

Little Red Riding Hood: A Newfangled Prairie Tale by Lisa Campbell Ernst. Simon & Schuster, 1995. In a twist to the original tale, granny makes an honest "man" out of the big bad wolf.

Corduroy by Don Freeman. Penguin Putnam, 1972. A bear's hopes come true when a little girl buys him and takes him home.

Three Little Kittens by Paul Galdone. Clarion Books, 1986. Three little kittens' adventures revolve around their mittens.

The Little Red Hen by Paul Galdone. Scholastic, 1973. A hen's lazy friends will not help her work so they receive none of her bread.

Whistle For Willie by Ezra Jack Keats. Viking, 1998. Peter learns to whistle.

The Carrot Seed by Ruth Krauss. Harper Festival, 1993. A little boy waits patiently for his carrot seed to grow.

If You Give a Mouse a Cookie by Laura Joffe Numeroff. HarperCollins, 1985. Giving a mouse a cookie leads him to ask for many things to go with that cookie.

The Rainbow Fish by Marcus Pfister. North-South Books, 1992. A fish learns the joy of sharing.

Curious George by H. A. Rey. Houghton Mifflin Co., 1976. A monkey's curiosity leads to many adventures.

Where the Wild Things Are by Maurice Sendak. Harper Festival, 1992. A boy takes an imaginary trip to where the wild things live.

The Cat in the Hat by Dr. Seuss. Random House, 1997. A troublesome cat makes mischief until he sees the lady of the house returning home.

Caps for Sale by Esphyr Slobodkina. HarperCollins, 1987. A cap peddler loses his caps to monkeys.

Tuesday by David Wiesner. Clarion Books, 1991. Frogs explore nearby houses via lily pads that float through the air.

Picture Detective—Clue Sheet

If You Give a Mouse a Cookie	*Caps for Sale*	Corduroy	*Curious George*
Clifford the Big Red Dog	**The Very Hungry Caterpillar**	**Where the Wild Things Are**	**The Little Red Hen**
Tuesday	**Little Red Riding Hood: A Newfangled Prairie Tale**	**The Carrot Seed**	**Five Little Monkeys Jumping on the Bed**
Do You Want to Be My Friend?	**Three Little Pigs**	**Three Little Kittens**	**Whistle for Willie**
Are You My Mother?	**The Rainbow Fish**	**The Cat in the Hat**	**Arthur Goes to Camp**

Boards Up!

Purpose

To introduce children to chapter books and to review Junie B. Jones books.

To Make

Draw a tally grid on the chalkboard, as shown below:

Team 1	Team 2	Team 3	Team 4	Team 5

Prepare questions relating to the Junie B. Jones books that have been read to the class (see sample questions on page 43).

You will need five individual chalkboards, five pieces of chalk and five erasers.

⏰ Preparation time—30 minutes

To Play

Divide the class into five teams. Give each team a chalkboard, eraser and chalk. Tell the students that the team members will take turns recording their answers on the chalkboard, with each member recording two answers.

Read a question. Have the team members confer on the answer. The recorder writes the team's answer, using a, b or c, on the chalkboard. Slowly count to 20, then say, "Boards Up!" The team recorders lift their chalkboards to reveal their team's answer. No more changes are allowed at this point.

Each correct answer gets a point. Tally the points on the grid. Continue until all of the questions have been asked. The team with the most points wins the game.

Books to Use

Junie B. Jones Smells Something Fishy by Barbara Park. Random House, 1998. Junie B. struggles to find a pet for pet day.

Junie B. Jones and the Stupid Smelly Bus by Barbara Park. Random House, 1992. Junie B. decides to hide at school rather than ride the scary bus home.

Sample Questions for Boards Up!

1. Who is the author of the Junie B. Jones books?
   a. Eric Carle   *b. Barbara Park*   c. Bill Martin

2. Who is the illustrator of the Junie B. Jones books?
   a. Joy Cowley   b. Barbara Park   *c. Denise Brunkus*

3. Who is Mrs.?
   a. the teacher   b. the principal   c. the nurse

4. What does the B. stand for?
   a. Barbie   *b. Beatrice*   c. Beth

5. What grade is Junie B. Jones in?
   a. first   b. second   *c. kindergarten*

6. How old is Junie B.?
   a. almost 6   b. almost 5   c. almost 7

7. What was on Junie B.'s hat the first day of school?
   a. a bull's head   b. frog eyes   *c. devil horns*

8. Why didn't Junie B. want to ride the school bus?
   a. she was afraid   b. she got motion sickness   c. her backpack was too heavy

9. Who does Junie B. hate?
   a. William   b. Warren   *c. Jim*

10. Where did Junie B. hide so she wouldn't have to ride the stupid, smelly bus home?
    a. in the closet   b. in the teachers' lounge   c. under the hallway stairs

11. What was Junie B.'s "MERGENCY"?
    a. she fell off the crutches   b. she cut her finger   *c. she had to use the potty*

12. Who was Noodle?
    a. a worm   b. a fish   c. a raccoon

13. What did Junie B. put on Sparkle's head?
    a. a rope   *b. Tickle's dog leash*   c. a cap

14. What did Junie B. take to school for pet day?
    a. a hot dog   b. a Kit Kat bar   *c. a fish stick*

15. What award did Fish Stick receive?
    a. most well-behaved   b. bubbliest   c. talkiest

16. Who called Junie B. a "Goonie Bird"?
    a. handsome Warren   *b. meanie Jim*   c. that Grace

Write-On, Junie B.

Purpose

To introduce children to chapter books and to review Junie B. Jones books.

To Make

Copy the stubby pencils from pages 45–48. Cut them out and paste them around the outside edges of a piece of poster board, see the sample game board below. Write the title "Write-On, Junie B." in the center of the board.

You will need clothespins, large clips or clamps to use as markers and a spinner or die to determine the number of moves.

Copy the Uh-oh cards and the bonus cards from pages 49–54 onto card stock. Laminate them, then cut them out.

🕑 Preparation time—45 minutes

To Play

Place the Uh-oh cards in one stack. Place the bonus cards in another stack.

Divide the class into two teams. Ask one team a question about Junie B. (use the questions on page 43 or make up your own). If the team answers correctly, they spin the spinner or throw the die. The team moves their marker the correct number of spaces. If the marker lands on an Uh-oh pencil or a bonus (*) pencil, the player must draw a card from the appropriate stack and follow the directions on the card. If the team answers incorrectly, move on to the other team. The first team to reach pencil 21 wins.

Books to Use

Any of the Junie B. Jones series by Barbara Park.

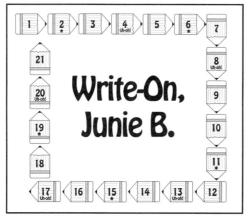

sample game board

13
Uh-oh!

14

15
*

16

17
Uh-oh!

18

UH-OH!

Junie B. jumps out of her seat and shouts in class. Go back 2 pencils.

UH-OH!

Junie B. hides from Mrs., and from Mr. Woo. Go back 3 pencils.

UH-OH!

Junie B. makes a face at that mean Jim. Go back 1 pencil.

UH-OH!

Junie B. hollers, "Watch it, you dumb Jim!" Go back 2 pencils.

UH-OH!

Junie B. yells in the library. Go back 1 pencil.

UH-OH!

Junie B. made a fist at the boy she can beat up. Go back 3 pencils.

UH-OH!

Junie B. calls principal "Baldy." Go back 1 pencil.

UH-OH!

Junie B. peeks her head in the boys' bathroom. Go back 2 pencils.

UH-OH!

Junie B. sticks one of Mrs.' gold stars on her forehead. Go back 3 pencils.

UH-OH!

Junie B. scribbles on the chalkboard. Go back 1 pencil.

UH-OH!

Junie B. climbs on a chair and peeks out the window. Go back 2 pencils.

UH-OH!

Junie B. makes peeky holes with the library books. Go back 1 pencil.

UH-OH!

Junie B. stirs the fish in the fish tank with her pencil. Go back 2 pencils.

UH-OH!

Junie B. puts crayons in the pencil sharpener. Go back 3 pencils.

UH-OH!

Junie B. breaks the electric pencil sharpener. Go back 1 pencil.

UH-OH!

Junie B. dumps out Nurse's Band-Aids. Go back 2 pencils.

UH-OH!

Junie B. puts on Nurse's purple sweater. Go back 1 pencil.

UH-OH!

Junie B. dangles on Nurse's crutches. Go back 1 pencil.

UH-OH!

Junie B. calls 911 because she has to go to the potty. Go back 3 pencils.

UH-OH!

Junie B. puts a potato on Twitter's head. Go back 3 pencils.

UH-OH!

Junie B. yells in the jar at Noodle. Go back 1 pencil.

UH-OH!

Junie B. puts a dog leash on Sparkle, the dead fish. Go back 2 pencils.

Write-On, Junie B.—Bonus Cards

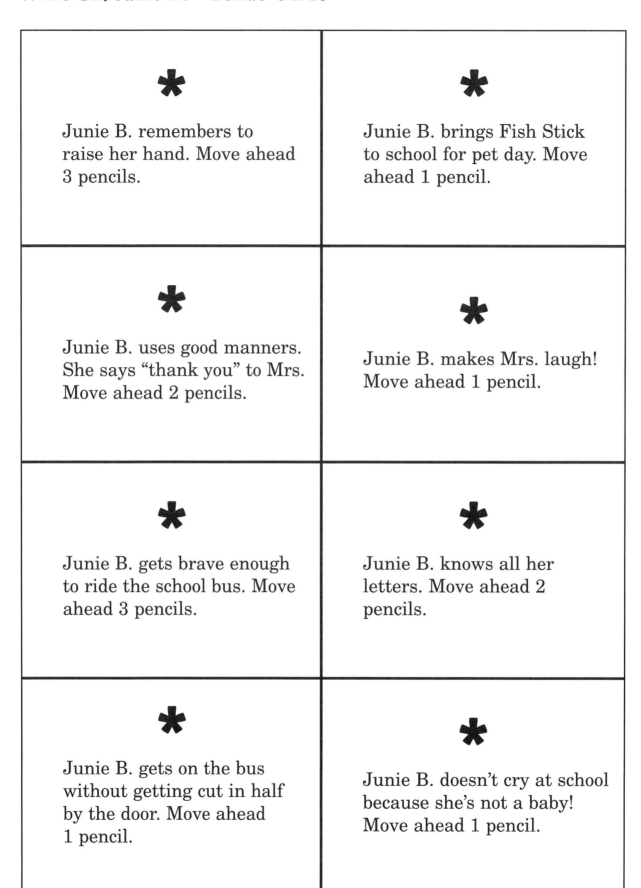

* Junie B. remembers to raise her hand. Move ahead 3 pencils.

* Junie B. brings Fish Stick to school for pet day. Move ahead 1 pencil.

* Junie B. uses good manners. She says "thank you" to Mrs. Move ahead 2 pencils.

* Junie B. makes Mrs. laugh! Move ahead 1 pencil.

* Junie B. gets brave enough to ride the school bus. Move ahead 3 pencils.

* Junie B. knows all her letters. Move ahead 2 pencils.

* Junie B. gets on the bus without getting cut in half by the door. Move ahead 1 pencil.

* Junie B. doesn't cry at school because she's not a baby! Move ahead 1 pencil.

Junie B. sits in the yellow chair, even though she wants to sit in the red one. Move ahead 2 pencils.

Junie B. knows how to write her name. Move ahead 3 pencils.

Junie B. gets a happy-face sticker on the drawing of her family. Move ahead 3 pencils.

Junie B. takes a quick drink so her friends can have a turn at the water fountain. Move ahead 2 pencils.

Junie B. remembers NOT to go in the boys' bathroom. Move ahead 1 pencil.

Nobody pours chocolate milk on Junie B.'s head. Move ahead 1 pencil.

Junie B. tells herself a story and makes herself feel better. Move ahead 3 pencils.

Junie B. remembers not to run in the hall. Move ahead 2 pencils.

Write-On, Junie B.—Bonus Cards

Junie B. has an emergency and calls 911. Move ahead 2 pencils.

Junie B. makes a new friend. Move ahead 2 pencils.

Junie B. is only in kindergarten and knows how to spell "B-A-B-Y." Move ahead 1 pencil.

Yeah! Junie B. gets to go outside for recess! Move ahead 3 pencils.

Junie B. finds her furry mittens. Move ahead 1 pencil.

Pickin' Time

Purpose

To review Eric Carle picture books and to promote interest in reading various books written by the same author.

To Make

Copy the apple tree game board from page 56 onto poster board. Color the tree if you wish. Laminate the tree, then make a hook on the top of each apple. To do this, push a paper fastener through the back of each apple. On the front of the apple, press the clip into a hook.

Copy the apple game cards from pages 57–59 onto red paper. Laminate the apples, then cut them out. Punch a hole in the top of each apple.

You will need one die.

⏰ Preparation time—60 minutes

To Play

Post the game board in front of the class. Match the numbers on the apple game cards to the numbers on the tree. Hang the game cards on the hooks.

Divide the class into two teams. Ask a member of the first team to roll the die. The team member "picks" the apple that matches the number on the die. Read the question aloud. If the team member correctly answers the question, the team gets to keep the apple. If they answer incorrectly, hang the apple back on the tree. If a six is rolled, the team loses its turn. If all of the apples for a number have been "picked," the team also loses its turn.

Have the teams take turns. The team with the most apples wins the game.

Books to Use

Do You Want to Be My Friend? by Eric Carle. HarperCollins, 1995. A little mouse searches for a friend.

The Grouchy Ladybug by Eric Carle. HarperCollins, 1999. A grouchy ladybug learns to share.

A House for Hermit Crab by Eric Carle. Simon & Schuster, 1991. As a hermit crab grows, he must find new homes.

Today Is Monday by Eric Carle. Philomel Books, 2001. Animals gather a feast for children to eat.

The Very Hungry Caterpillar by Eric Carle. Philomel Books, 1987. A caterpillar eats many things on its way to becoming a butterfly.

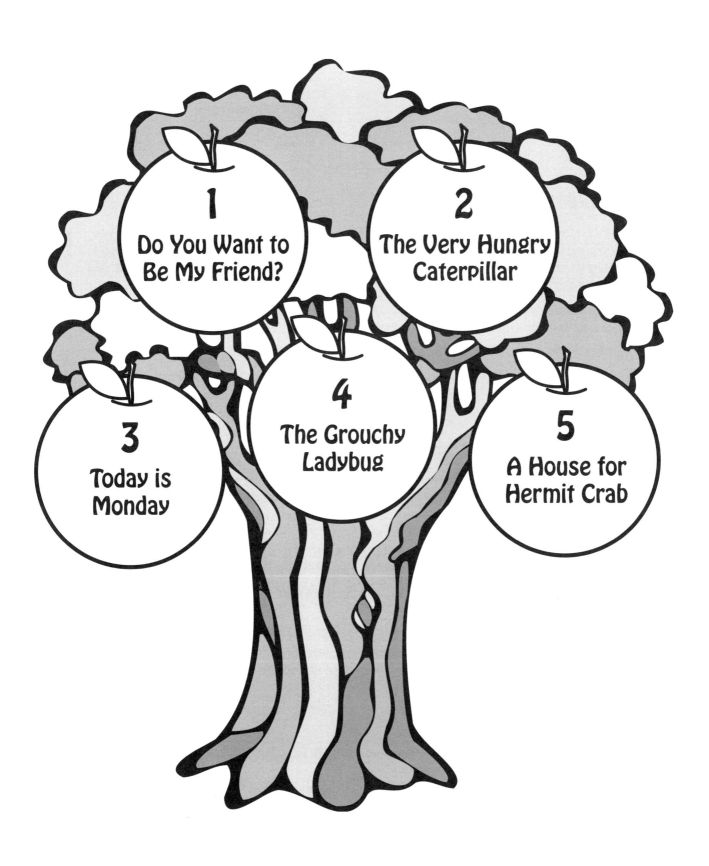

1

What animal wanted a friend?

1

Which animal had a golden mane?

1

Who walked on his hands?

1

Did the fox want to be mouse's friend?

1

What was in the kangaroo's pouch?

1

Who said, "Yes, I will be your friend"?

2

Where was the egg laying?

2

What came out of the egg?

2

What did the caterpillar look for when he popped out of the egg?

2

Why did the caterpillar get a stomachache?

2

What did the caterpillar eat to make his stomach feel better?

2

What did the caterpillar change into?

Pickin' Time—Apples

3
What did the snake eat?

3
Who ate zoooop?

3
Who ate ice cream?

3
Who ate the chicken?

3
Who ate ALL the food?

4
When did fireflies dance around the moon?

4
What did the ladybugs want for breakfast?

4
Who said, "Want to fight?"

4
Why did the grouchy ladybug always say, "Oh, you're not big enough"?

4
What animal's tail gave the ladybug a big slap?

5
Why did Hermit Crab have to move?

5
Where did Hermit Crab live?

5
Why did Hermit Crab put sea anemones on his new shell?

5
How did the lantern fish help Hermit Crab?

5
Who moved into Hermit Crab's beautifully decorated shell?

Answers to Apple Cards

Do You Want to Be My Friend?

What animal wanted a friend? *(mouse)*

Which animal had a golden mane? *(lion)*

Who walked on his hands? *(monkey)*

Did the fox want to be mouse's friend? *(no)*

What was in the kangaroo's pouch? *(baby)*

Who said, "Yes, I will be your friend"? *(mouse)*

The Very Hungry Caterpillar

Where was the egg laying? *(on a leaf)*

What came out of the egg? *(caterpillar)*

What did the caterpillar look for when he popped out of the egg? *(food)*

Why did the caterpillar get a stomachache? *(he ate too much)*

What did the caterpillar eat to make his stomach feel better? *(green leaf)*

What did the caterpillar change into? *(butterfly)*

Today Is Monday

What did the snake eat? *(spaghetti)*

Who ate zoooop? *(elephant)*

Who ate ice cream? *(monkey)*

Who ate the chicken? *(fox)*

Who ate ALL the food? *(children)*

The Grouchy Ladybug

When did fireflies dance around the moon? *(night)*

What did the ladybugs want for breakfast? *(aphids)*

Who said, "Want to fight?" *(grouchy ladybug)*

Why did the grouchy ladybug always say, "Oh, you're not big enough"? *(he was afraid to fight)*

What animal's tail gave the ladybug a big slap? *(whale)*

A House for Hermit Crab

Why did Hermit Crab have to move? *(he was too big for his shell)*

Where did Hermit Crab live? *(ocean floor)*

Why did Hermit Crab put sea anemones on his new shell? *(to decorate it)*

How did the lantern fish help Hermit Crab? *(he lit up his house)*

Who moved into Hermit Crab's beautifully decorated shell? *(little crab)*

Cover-Up

Purpose

To review Eric Carle picture books as well as author, character, setting, illustrator, beginning, middle and end.

To Make

Enlarge the game board on page 65 by 115%. Make seven copies on poster board. Laminate them.

Make a copy of the game cards on pages 61–64. Laminate them and cut them apart.

⏰ Preparation time—20 minutes

To Play

Divide the students into six teams. Give each team a game board and keep the last game board with you. Stack all of the game cards in the appropriate boxes on your game board.

Ask a member of Team 1 to come select a game card from your game board. Read the question aloud. Team 1 has 30 seconds to answer the question. If they answer correctly, they put the game card in the appropriate box on their game board. If they do not answer within the 30 seconds or answer incorrectly, return the game card to the bottom of the stack.

Continue with Team 2 and so on. The first team to cover-up, or have one game card under each title on their game board, wins.

1 Who is the author?	**1** Who is the illustrator?
1 Who is the main character?	**1** What is the setting of the story?
1 Did Mouse ask Peacock to be his friend at the beginning, middle or end of the story?	**1** What happened at the end of the story?
1 Did Mouse ask Horse to be his friend at the beginning, middle or end of the story?	**1** Name a character, other than the mouse, found in this book.
2 Who is the main character?	**2** Who is the author?
2 Who is the illustrator?	**2** What is the setting of the story?

Cover-Up—Game Cards

2 Who is the biggest character in the book?	**2** Did the grouchy ladybug ask the boa constrictor to fight at the beginning, middle or end of the story?
2 Who said, "Want to fight?"	**2** Name a character, other than the grouchy ladybug, found in this book.
2 What happened at the end of the story?	**3** What is the setting of the story?
3 Name two characters in the book.	**3** Who ate the food at the end of the story?
3 What food did the cat carry in the middle of the book?	**3** Who is the author?
3 Who is the illustrator?	**3** What food did Porcupine carry at the beginning of the book?

4 Who is the main character?	**4** Did the caterpillar eat lots of food at the beginning, middle or end of the story?
4 What is the setting of the story?	**4** Did the caterpillar turn into a butterfly at the beginning, middle or end of the story?
4 Who is the author?	**4** Who is the illustrator?
4 Was the caterpillar an egg at the beginning, middle or end of the story?	**5** Who is the author?
5 Who is the illustrator?	**5** Who lit up Hermit Crab's house?
5 In the middle of the story, Hermit Crab invited sea creatures to live on his house. Why?	**5** Why did Hermit Crab move out of his shell at the end of the book?

Cover-Up—Game Cards and Answers

5 At the beginning of the story, Hermit Crab had to move. Why?	5 What is the setting of the story?

Answers to Game Cards

Do You Want to Be My Friend?

Who is the author/illustrator? *(Eric Carle)*

Who is the main character? *(mouse)*

What is the setting of the story? *(jungle, zoo, etc.)*

Did Mouse ask Peacock to be his friend at the beginning, middle or end of the story? *(middle)*

What happened at the end of the story? *(a small gray mouse became Mouse's friend)*

Did Mouse ask Horse to be his friend at the beginning, middle or end of the story? *(beginning)*

Name a character, other than the mouse, found in this book. *(horse, crocodile, lion, hippo, seal, monkey, peacock, fox, kangaroo, giraffe, snake)*

The Grouchy Ladybug

Who is the main character? *(grouchy ladybug)*

Who is the author/illustrator? *(Eric Carle)*

What is the setting of the story? *(leaf, ocean, etc.)*

Who is the biggest character in the book? *(whale)*

Did the grouchy ladybug ask the boa constrictor to fight at the beginning, middle or end of the story? *(middle)*

Who said, "Want to fight?" *(grouchy ladybug)*

Name a character, other than the grouchy ladybug, found in this book. *(friendly ladybug, yellow jacket, beetle, praying mantis, sparrow, lobster, skunk, boa, hyena, gorilla, rhino, elephant, whale)*

What happened at the end of the story? *(grouchy ladybug shared aphids with friendly ladybug)*

Today Is Monday

What is the setting of the story? *(outdoors, dining room, etc.)*

Name two characters in the book. *(porcupine, boa, elephant, cat, pelican, fox, monkey, parrot, children)*

Who ate the food at the end of the story? *(the children)*

What food did the cat carry in the middle of the book? *(roast beef)*

Who is the author/illustrator? *(Eric Carle)*

What food did Porcupine carry at the beginning of the book? *(green bean)*

The Very Hungry Caterpillar

Who is the main character? *(caterpillar)*

Did the caterpillar eat lots of food at the beginning, middle or end of the story? *(middle)*

What is the setting of the story? *(leaf, garden, etc.)*

Did the caterpillar turn into a butterfly at the beginning, middle or end of the story? *(end)*

Who is the author/illustrator? *(Eric Carle)*

Was the caterpillar an egg at the beginning, middle or end of the story? *(beginning)*

A House for Hermit Crab

Who is the author/illustrator? *(Eric Carle)*

Who lit up Hermit Crab's house? *(lantern fish)*

In the middle of the story, Hermit Crab invited sea creatures to live on his house. Why? *(to decorate it)*

Why did Hermit Crab move out of his shell at the end of the book? *(he was too big for his shell)*

At the beginning of the story, Hermit Crab had to move. Why? *(he was too big for his shell)*

What is the setting of the story? *(sea floor, ocean)*

**1
Do You Want to
Be My Friend?**

game cards

**4
The Very Hungry
Caterpillar**

game cards

**2
The Grouchy
Ladybug**

game cards

**3
Today Is Monday**

game cards

**5
A House for
Hermit Crab**

game cards

Caldecott Ping-Pong

Purpose

To review Caldecott Medal winners.

To Make

Copy the game sheet from page 67. Cut the titles into strips.

⏰ Preparation time—15 minutes

To Play

Divide the class into two teams. Give each player a title strip.

Direct a member of one team to read a title to the other team. The other team tries to fill in the missing word. If they answer correctly, no team receives a point. If they answer incorrectly, the team reading the title gets a point. Do not give the correct answer at this time since the title may be used for a later turn.

Have the teams take turns until all of the titles have been completed. Count the points. The team with the most points wins.

Answers: *Why Mosquitoes **Buzz** in People's Ears; Where the **Wild** Things Are; The Snowy **Day**; Make Way for **Ducklings**; Officer Buckle and **Gloria**; Madeline's **Rescue**; Grandfather's **Journey**; Mirette on the **High** Wire; The **Funny** Little Woman; Song and **Dance** Man; Polar **Express**; Sylvester and the **Magic** Pebble; A Story, **A Story**; Joseph Had a Little **Overcoat**; **Lon** Po Po; The **Little** House; **Abraham** Lincoln; The **Biggest** Bear; Owl **Moon**; Nine Days to **Christmas***

Why Mosquitoes _____ in People's Ears

Where the _____ Things Are

The Snowy _____

Make Way for _____

Officer Buckle and _____

Madeline's _____

Grandfather's _____

Mirette on the _____ Wire

The _____ Little Woman

Song and _____ Man

Polar _____

Sylvester and the _____ Pebble

A Story, _____

Joseph Had a Little _____

_____ Po Po

The _____ House

_____ Lincoln

The _____ Bear

Owl _____

Nine Days to _____

Find Your Match

Purpose

To review easy fiction call numbers.

To Make

Cut 13 pieces of 8½" x 11" paper in half. On each piece of paper, write a title with the author's name (see samples on page 69). Write the corresponding call number on another piece of paper. The call numbers should be written large enough so they can be seen at a distance. There should be 13 call number sheets and 13 title/author sheets (enough for 26 students).

⏰ Preparation time—20 minutes

To Play

Divide the class into two teams. Hand out one sheet to each student. Have the students hold their sheets so everyone can see the information.

Have one team member look for his or her match (i.e., title/author sheet to call number sheet). If the player correctly finds the match, he or she claims the sheet for his or her team.

Have each team take turns. The game ends when all of the sheets have been correctly matched. The team with the most matches wins the game.

Find Your Match—Sample Titles/Authors and Call Numbers

Where the Wild Things Are by Maurice Sendak — **E Sen**

Tuesday by David Wiesner — **E Wie**

The Grouchy Ladybug by Eric Carle — **E Car**

Curious George by H. A. Rey — **E Rey**

Dear Mr. Blueberry by Simon James — **E Jam**

The Rainbow Fish by Marcus Pfister — **E Pfi**

The Kissing Hand by Audrey Penn — **E Pen**

Stellaluna by Janell Cannon — **E Can**

Max's Dragon Shirt by Rosemary Wells — **E Wel**

Corduroy by Don Freeman — **E Fre**

Hooway For Wodney Wat by Helen Lester — **E Les**

The Napping House by Audrey Wood — **E Woo**

Dragon Gets By by Dav Pilkey — **E Pil**

What's in Katy's Pockets?

Purpose

A game to use as a follow-up activity with the picture book *Katy No-Pocket.*

To give children practice using descriptive words.

To Make

Make 20 copies of the pocket from page 76 onto card stock. Number the pockets, then color and decorate each one differently. Glue the pockets in numerical order onto poster board, but leave the top of the pocket open. Laminate the pockets and slit open the top edge of each one so you can slide an animal card inside.

Copy and cut out the animal cards from pages 73–75. Match the animals with their clue numbers from pages 71–72 and place the appropriate animal card in the corresponding pocket.

⏰ Preparation time—1 hour

To Play

Tell the class that Katy's Pockets have animals inside them. Everyone will have a chance to guess what the animals are.

Ask a student to choose a pocket. Read the animal clue from pages 71–72 for that pocket. If the student guesses the animal correctly, he or she gets to pull the animal out of the pocket and keep it.

Continue until each child has had a turn.

Note: *If you prefer to make the animals permanent, copy, color and laminate them. Have the children pull the animals from the pockets, but return them at the end of the game.*

Books to Use

Katy No-Pocket by Emmy Payne. Houghton Mifflin, 1972. A pouch-less mother kangaroo finds a unique way to carry her baby and other animals as well.

See page 77 for other kangaroo-related stories.

What's in Katy's Pockets?—Animal Clues

1. This animal ...
   ... gives us milk
   ... has an udder
   ... says "moo"
   (cow)

2. This animal ...
   ... has wings and feathers
   ... has a comb on its head
   ... says "cluck, cluck"
   ... lives in a coop
   (chicken)

3. This animal ...
   ... has a mane
   ... lets people ride on its back
   ... has four hooves
   ... says "neigh"
   (horse)

4. This animal ...
   ... has a snout
   ... likes mud
   ... lives in a pen or sty
   ... says "oink"
   (pig)

5. This animal ...
   ... is covered with fluffy wool
   ... is usually white
   ... says "baa"
   (sheep)

6. This animal ...
   ... is a bird we eat on
      Thanksgiving Day
   ... says "gobble, gobble"
   (turkey)

7. This animal ...
   ... has fins and scales
   ... swims in the water
   ... breathes through gills
   (fish)

8. This animal ...
   ... is in a story with Goldilocks
   ... growls
   ... lives in the woods
   ... is the same kind of animal as
      Winnie the Pooh
   (bear)

9. This animal ...
   ... carries its shell on its back
   ... moves very slowly
   ... is the same kind of animal as
      Franklin
   (turtle)

10. This animal ...
   ... lives in the ocean
   ... has eight long legs
   ... gave wise advice to the
      Rainbow Fish
   (octopus)

11. This animal ...
   ... lives in the ocean
   ... has very sharp teeth
   ... eats other fish and even people
   (shark)

12. This animal ...
   ... has two horns and will butt
      people
   ... eats almost anything
   ... walked over the troll's bridge
   (goat)

What's in Katy's Pockets?—Animal Clues

13. This animal ...
   ... is a good pet
   ... walks beside you on a leash
   ... likes to be petted
   ... says "wuff, wuff"
(dog)

14. This animal ...
   ... is a good swimmer
   ... says "quack, quack"
   ... has webbed feet
(duck)

15. This animal ...
   ... is a good pet
   ... has claws
   ... has soft fur
   ... purrs and says "meow"
(cat)

16. This animal ...
   ... likes the water
   ... has long back legs
   ... is often green
   ... has big eyes that pop out
   ... says "croak" or "ribbit"
(frog)

17. This animal ...
   ... tried to eat Little Red Riding Hood
   ... has very sharp teeth
   ... looks like a dog
(wolf)

18. This animal ...
   ... has a pouch to carry her baby
   ... is the same kind of animal as Katy No-Pocket
(kangaroo)

19. This animal ...
   ... has a long trunk
   ... is very huge
   ... has two tusks
(elephant)

20. This animal ...
   ... has black stripes on an orange body
   ... lives in the jungle
   ... is a cat
(tiger)

21. This animal ...
   ... has a mane if it is a male
   ... is called "king of the jungle"
   ... roars
(lion)

22. This animal ...
   ... swings in trees using its tail
   ... lives in the jungle
   ... uses its front feet like hands
(monkey)

23. This animal ...
   ... looks like a horse
   ... has black and white stripes
   ... lives in Africa
(zebra)

24. This animal ...
   ... has a VERY long neck
   ... has brown spots on a yellow body
   ... lives in Africa
(giraffe)

What's in Katy's Pockets?—Animal Cards

What's in Katy's Pockets?—Animal Cards

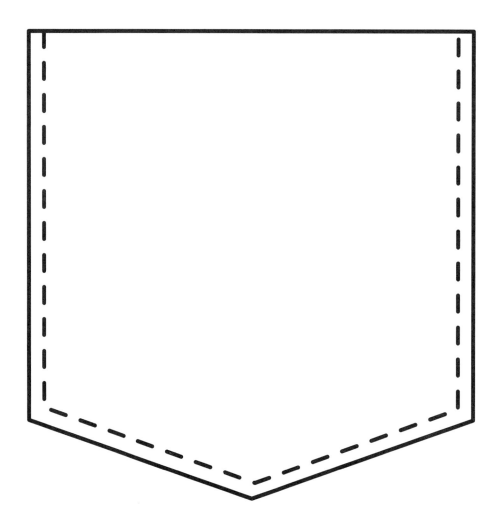

Hopping Around Australia

Purpose

To have students play a game as the culminating activity in a study of Australia.

To follow up a story that relates to Australia.

To Make

Photocopy the game board from page 78 onto poster board as it is or enlarge it by 115%. Laminate the game board.

You will need two different colored clothespins or clips for markers and a spinner or die to determine the number of moves.

⏰ Preparation time—30 minutes

To Play

Divide the class into two teams. Ask a player from one team a question about Australia (see sample questions on page 79). If the answer is correct, direct the player to spin the spinner or throw the die. Move that team's marker the appropriate number of spaces.

Have the teams take turns. The first team to reach the end is the winner.

Books to Use

The One in the Middle is the Green Kangaroo by Judy Blume. Dell, 1981. Being a green kangaroo in a play changes Freddy's feelings about being the middle child.

Kangaroos by Denise Burt. Carolrhoda Books, 2000. Text and photographs present the habits, life cycle and natural environment of the kangaroo.

Where Are You, Blue Kangaroo? by Emma Chichester Clark. Doubleday, 2001. Lily's blue kangaroo is distressed that she loses him so often.

Joey Runs Away by Jack Kent. Simon & Schuster, 1985. Joey leaves his mother to avoid cleaning her pouch, but eventually returns to the comfort of his home.

Australia by Sean McCollum. Carolrhoda Books, 1999. Includes "Fast Facts About Australia," information highlighted in caption, bibliography and glossary.

Australia by David Petersen. Children's Press, 1998. Primary-level book about Australia. Includes photographs, maps, on-line sites and "fast facts."

Joey: The Story of a Baby Kangaroo by Hope Ryden. Tambourine Books, 1994. A photo essay of the life of a joey and his encounters with other animals of Australia.

Kangaroos by John Woodward. Benchmark Books, 1997. Describes the physical characteristics, habitat and behavior of kangaroos living in Australia and New Guinea.

Hopping Around Australia—Game Board

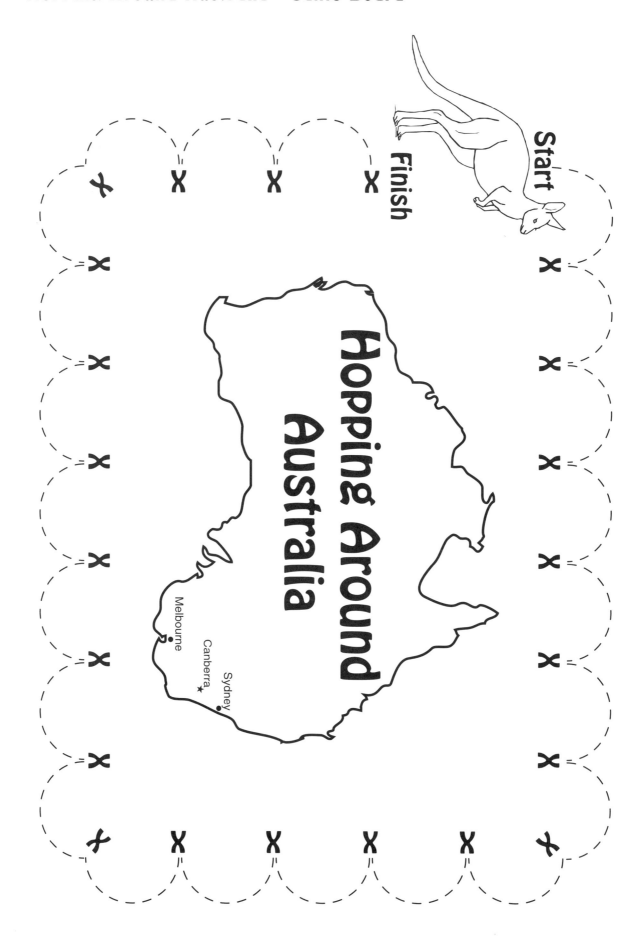

Start

Finish

Hopping Around Australia

Melbourne

Canberra

Sydney

Sample Questions About Australia

1. True or False? Australia is the only continent that is also one country. *(T)*

2. Australia is called the "Land Down Under." What is it down under? *(the equator)*

3. True or False? Australia is the second largest continent in the world. *(F)*

4. What language do most people in Australia speak? *(English)*

5. True or False? Sydney is the capital city of Australia. *(F)*

6. Who is the queen of Australia? *(Queen Elizabeth II)*

7. What season is December to February in Australia? *(summer)*

8. Which of these animals is not native to Australia:
    a. emu   *b. llama*   c. platypus

9. Which continent is larger: North America or Australia? *(North America)*

10. Which is not a marsupial?
    a. kangaroo   b. koala   *c. panda*

11. What season are June and July in Australia? *(winter)*

12. True or False? Australia is the largest producer of wool. *(T)*

13. What do kangaroos mostly eat? *(plants)*

14. True or False? The emu bird can soar higher than an eagle. *(F)*

15. True or False? The platypus not only lays eggs, has webbed feet and a duck-like bill, but is also a mammal. *(T)*

16. Which legs, the fore legs or the hind legs, does the kangaroo use to jump? *(hind legs)*

17. What is a joey? *(a baby kangaroo)*

18. A lift in Australia means a:
    a. kite   *b. elevator*   c. blimp

19. What is the Great Barrier Reef made of? *(coral)*

20. True or False? The outback is located beside the sea. *(F)*

21. True or False? Australia is located in the Atlantic Ocean. *(F)*

22. True or False? Australia has many deserts. *(T)*

Tangram Puzzle

Purpose

To follow up a story set in China or to use while studying China.

To Make

Make two copies of the tangram sheet from page 83 onto card stock. Cut the tangrams out and put the pieces for each tangram in a separate paper bag.

⏰ Preparation time—15 minutes

To Play

Divide the class into two teams. Give each team a paper bag. Direct the teams to select one person to put the puzzle together.

Ask a player from one team a question related to China (see the sample questions on page 82). If the player gives the correct answer, he or she reaches into the team's bag, takes a puzzle piece and gives it to the player putting the puzzle together.

Have the teams take turns. The first team to put their tangram together wins.

Books to Use

The Empty Pot by Demi. Henry Holt and Company, 1990. A young boy is declared to be worthy of being an emperor because of his honesty.

Happy New Year! Kung-hsi Fa-ts'ai! by Demi. Crown, 1997. Examines the customs, traditions, foods and lore associated with the celebration of the Chinese New Year.

Count Your Way Through China by James Haskins. Lerner Publishing Group, 1997. The author uses the numbers one through ten, written in Chinese, to highlight concepts about China and Chinese culture.

Two of Everything: A Chinese Folktale by Lily Toy Hong. Albert Whitman & Co., 1993. A magic brass pot, found by Mr. Haktak, causes problems because of its magical power to duplicate whatever is dropped into the pot.

Ming Lo Moves the Mountain by Arnold Lobel. Morrow, 1993. Ming Lo seeks the advice of the village wise man on how to move the mountain next to his house.

China by Janet Riehecky. Carolrhoda Books, 1999. Examines the history, society, economy and culture of China.

Pandas by Gillian Standring. Bookwright Press, 1991. Looks at the physical characteristics, behavior and life cycle of the panda in the wild and in captivity. Focuses on efforts to save this endangered species from extinction.

The Chinese Siamese Cat by Amy Tan. Macmillan, 1994. Ming Miao tells her kittens about the antics of one of their ancestors, Sagwa of China, that produced the unusual markings they have had for thousands of years.

Grandfather Tang's Story by Ann Tompert. Crown, 1990. Grandfather Tang uses tangrams to tell a tale of two foxes who change their shapes to avoid danger.

Lon Po Po: A Red-Riding Hood Story From China by Ed Young. Philomel Books, 1996. Three sisters staying home alone are endangered by a hungry wolf that is disguised as their grandmother.

Sample Questions About China

1. China is the world's
   a. largest country in land size
   b. second largest country in land size
   c. third largest country in land size

2. China is part of what continent? *(Asia)*

3. The three seas that touch China are part of what ocean? *(Pacific)*

4. Which is not in China?
   a. Nile River   b. Gobi Desert   c. Yangtze River

5. Which is the capital city of China?
   a. Tokyo   *b. Beijing*   c. Bangkok

6. True or False? Hong Kong is part of China. *(T)*

7. The Great Wall is almost
   a. 1,000 miles long   b. 2,500 miles long   *c. 4,000 miles*

8. The Chinese money is called
   a. yen   *b. yuan*   c. pesos

9. True or False? The Chinese New Year is not on January 1. *(T)*

10. What is the main food of the giant panda? *(bamboo)*

11. The Chinese were the first to make silk. Where does the silk fiber come from? *(cocoon of the silkworm)*

12. What is the purpose of the abacus? *(to do mathematics)*

13. Which is not true of China?
    a. China has the most people of any country in the world.
    b. China has the world's highest mountain peak.
    c. China has the longest river in the world.

14. True or False? Paper was invented in China. *(T)*

15. True or False? The official name for China is the People's Republic of China. *(T)*

16. Where is the Forbidden City?
    a. Beijing   b. Tokyo   c. Honolulu

17. China has
    a. 50 million people   *b. over 1 billion people*   c. 250 million people

18. Which river is in China?
    a. Amazon River   b. Nile River   *c. Yellow River*

19. What is another name for table tennis? *(Ping-Pong)*

20. In the past, who ruled China?
    a. emperor   b. king   c. president

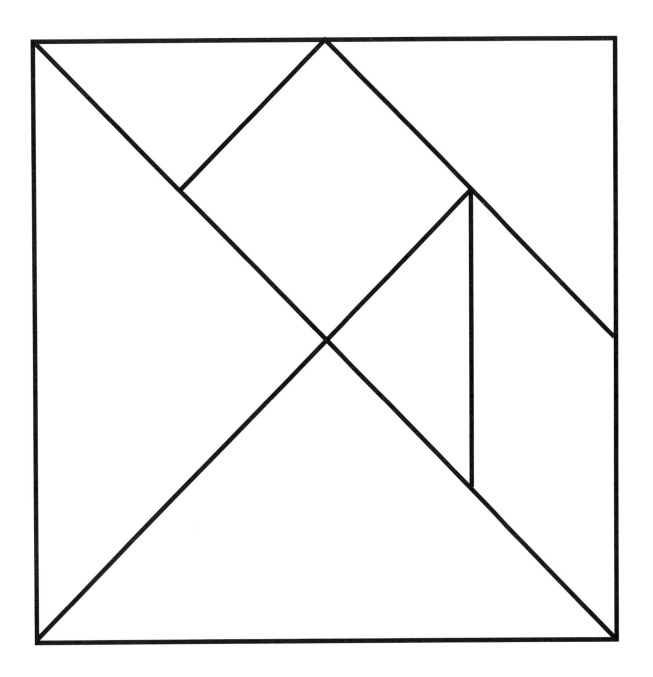

Reach the Poles

Purpose

To use with a story related to an animal of the polar regions or to use while studying the polar regions.

To Make

Copy one score sheet from page 88 for each team.

You will need a spinner or die and markers such as beans, buttons or small card-stock squares.

You will also need a story that is set in a polar region.

⏰ Preparation time—10 minutes

To Play

Read the story. Divide the class into two teams. Have each team designate a scorekeeper.

Ask a player from one team a question about the polar regions (see the sample questions on pages 86–87). If the answer is correct, the player spins the spinner or throws the die. The team's scorekeeper moves the marker the appropriate number of jumps.

Have the teams take turns. The object of the first game is to be the first to reach the North Pole (from the bottom to the top of the score sheet).

When the first game is completed, start the second game with the losing team answering the first question. The object of the second game is to be the first team to reach the South Pole.

Books to Use

Polar Lands by Norman Barrett. Franklin Watts, 1989. Describes the life and climate of the polar regions, research being done there and the possible future of these regions.

Little Polar Bear and the Brave Little Hare by Hans de Beer. North-South Books, 1998. Lars, a polar bear, befriends a lost hare.

The Practically Perfect Pajamas by Erik Brooks. Winslow Press, 2000. A polar bear gives up his beloved footed pajamas after the other polar bears tease him about them, but then he realizes how useful they were.

A Sled Dog for Moshi by Jeanne Bushey. Hyperion Books for Children, 1994. Moshi learns the value of a sled dog when caught in a snowstorm.

A for Antarctica by Jonathan Chester. Tricycle Press, 1995. With full-color photos and informative, easy-to-read text, this adventurous alphabet book takes young explorers far away to find out what it's really like—and what it takes to survive—in the frozen land at the "bottom" of the world.

Antarctica by Helen Cowcher. Farrar, Straus & Giroux, 1990. The beautiful ice world of the penguins and seals is interrupted by metal enemies made by man.

The Arctic Son by Jean Craighead George. Hyperion Books for Children, 1997. A young boy learns about life in the Arctic from his Eskimo friends.

The World of Polar Bears by Virginia Harrison. Gareth Stevens Inc., 1989. Describes in brief text and illustrations the lives of polar bears in their natural settings showing how they feed, defend themselves and breed.

Tacky the Penguin by Helen Lester. Houghton Mifflin, 1990. Tacky's perfect friends find him annoying until his odd behavior saves the day.

White Bear, Ice Bear by Joanne Ryder. Morrow Junior Books, 1989. A boy is transformed into a polar bear and experiences the awakening, feeding and wandering of a polar bear from his own viewpoint.

Tiktala by Margaret Shaw-MacKinnon. Holiday House, 1996. When the spirit guide changes Tiktala into a seal, she learns the ways of seals and how harmful humans can be.

Polar Bear and Grizzly Bear by Rod Theodorou. Rigby Interactive Library, 1997. Compares and contrasts the physical attributes, habits and habitats of polar bears and grizzly bears.

Sample Questions for Reach the Poles

1. Which does not describe the polar lands?
   a. cold
   b. covered with ice and snow for most of the year
   c. near the equator

2. Which does describe the polar lands?
   a. around the earth's North and South poles
   b. tropical climate
   c. home of the flamingo bird

3. Which ocean is at the North Pole?
   a. Arctic   b. Pacific   c. Indian

4. Which continent is the South Pole on?   *(Antarctica)*

5. Which is not correct about the Arctic region?
   a. Eskimos live here.
   b. This is the windiest place on Earth.
   c. Many icebergs float here.

6. True or False? The Arctic and the Antarctic regions are known as the "Land of the Midnight Sun."   *(T)*

7. True or False? The sun never shines at the poles.   *(F)*

8. The polar lands are cold because
   a. the way the earth moves around the sun
   b. the sun never shines there
   c. the land is below sea level

9. True or False? Even though it is cold and often covered with snow, the Arctic area has some plant life.   *(T)*

10. True or False? There are active volcanoes in the Antarctic region.   *(T)*

11. True or False? Whales do not live in the Antarctic waters, because the water is too cold.   *(F)*

12. Who does not live in a rookery?
    a. bears   b. seals   c. penguins

13. True or False? Most Eskimos survive by hunting and fishing.   *(T)*

14. Adélies and Emperors are kinds of
    a. penguins   b. plants   c. seals

15. Who/what does not eat krill?
    a. whales   b. seals   *c. moss*

16. True or False? Part of the Arctic region is in one of our 50 states.   *(T)*

17. Describe a kayak.   *(a kind of canoe)*

18. True or False? The polar lands are rich in minerals.   *(T)*

19. True or False? Antarctica is the coldest place on Earth.   *(T)*

20. What transportation did Norwegian explorer Roald Amundsen use to reach the South Pole on Dec. 14, 1911?   *(dog-drawn sled)*

21. What is a husky?   *(a dog)*

22. True or False? The polar bear is the largest of all bears.   *(T)*

23. The polar bear is the predator of what animal?   *(the seal)*

24. Which country does the Arctic Circle touch?
    a. Mexico   *b. Canada*   c. Australia

25. Which is Antarctica closest to?
    a. South America   b. Canada   c. Hawaii

Reach the Poles—Score Sheet

Game 1—North Pole		Game 2—South Pole	
Team 1—End	Team 2—End	Team 1—Start	Team 2—Start
Team 1—Start	Team 2—Start	Team 1—End	Team 2—End

A Story, A Story Game

Purpose

To follow up *A Story, A Story* retold by Gail E. Haley.

To Make

Make two copies of the cards from pages 91–92 onto card stock. Cut them out. Keep the two sets of cards separate.

⏰ Preparation time—20 minutes

To Play

Read the book to the students.

Divide the class into two teams. Place the two stacks of cards face down on the table. The object of the game is to be the first to locate the three items that the Sky God requests for the box of stories.

Direct a player from one team to turn over a card. If the picture is one of the items (Osebo the leopard of-the-terrible-teeth, Mmboro the hornet who-stings-like-fire or Mmoatia the fairy whom-men-never-see), another player on the same team turns over a second card. If the picture is not one of the three items, the game continues with the other team taking a turn. When an item is located, that card is kept out until the end of the game.

Have the teams take turns until one team locates the three items.

Optional: You may ask players a question related to Africa or to the story (see sample questions on page 90). If the player's answer is correct, they may turn over a card.

Books to Use

A Story, A Story: An African Tale by Gail E. Haley. Aladdin Books, 1986. A Caldecott Award winning story about Ananse, the Spider man, who buys a golden box of stories from the Sky God.

Sample Questions for A Story, A Story Game

1. Who was Nyame?   *(Sky God)*

2. Where did Nyame, the Sky God, keep his golden box of stories?
    (by his side)

3. How did Ananse go to see the Sky God?   *(spider web)*

4. Where did this story come from?   *(Africa)*

5. What is the missing word: Osebo the leopard of-the-_____-teeth.
    (terrible)

6. What is the missing word: Mmboro the hornet who-_____-like-fire.
    (stings)

7. What is the missing word: Mmoatia the _____ whom-men-never-see.
    (fairy)

8. Ananse used the calabash with water to catch the _____.   *(hornets)*

9. What did Ananse put in the wooden doll's bowl?   *(yams)*

10. Why did the fairy get stuck to the wooden doll?   *(Ananse put sticky gum
    on it.)*

11. What is the name of the stories Ananse got from the Sky God?
    (Spider Stories)

12. What did Ananse do to the stories he got from the Sky God?
    (scatter them)

13. What kind of award did *A Story, A Story* receive?   *(Caldecott Medal)*

14. Is Ananse a fable, folktale or biography?   *(a folktale)*

15. Describe Ananse.   *(weak, old man, wise, brave)*

16. Where are the folktale books in the media center?   *(have student point to
    section)*

A Story, A Story Game—Game Cards

A—My Name Is Amazon

Purpose

To use with the study of the rain forest.

To Make

Make a copy of the vocabulary words on page 94 for each student.

Copy two sets of the alphabet cards on pages 95–96 onto card stock. Cut the cards out and put them in a paper bag.

⏲ Preparation time—At least a week for students to research the words on the list

⏲ Preparation time—15 to 20 minutes

To Play

Divide the class into teams of five students. Give each student a vocabulary list. Direct the teams to divide the responsibility of researching the unfamiliar words among their team members. Give the students time to research the words.

Provide time for the team members to share their research results with their teams.

Have a team member from the first team take an alphabet card. If the letter is an "A," a player from the team gives a term from the vocabulary list related to that letter. For example:

> **A**—My name is **Amazon** and I am a river in a rain forest.

> **B**—My name is **boa constrictor** and I am a snake in a rain forest.

If the response is correct, the team keeps the card. Each card is worth a point. If the response is incorrect, the other team may respond for a bonus point. If their response is correct, they continue, thus getting two turns in a row.

Have the teams take turns until all of the cards have been used. The team with the most points wins.

Words Related to the Rainforest

Please research any words that you do not know.

Amazon River	epiphytes	kinkajou	rat
anaconda	equator	liana	reserve
ant	fern	leopard	resin
anteater	fig	lichen	roots
armadillo	forest floor	macaw	salamander
bamboo	frog	mango	sloth
banana	fungi	margay	slug
basilisk	gibbon	marmoset	snake
boa constrictor	ginger	monkey	South America
Brazil	global warming	mushroom	spider monkey
butterfly	gorilla	nectar	tamarin
cacao	habitat	nitrogen	tapir
canopy	hibiscus	nutrient	tarantula
capybara	hog	nuts	toucan
carbon dioxide	honey creeper	ocelot	tree frog
chameleon	hummingbird	okapi	treetops
chimpanzee	iguana	opossum	vampire bat
civet	India	orchid	vines
coati	Indonesia	otter	vole
deer	insect	palm tree	wild pig
deforestation	jacana	parrot	wildlife
dolphin	jaguar	peccary	woodpecker
eagle	jungle	pineapple	
egret	kangaroo	poison dart frog	
elephant	kakapo	porcupine	
emergents	katydid	rainfall	

A	B	C
D **Double Point**	E	F
G	H	I
J **Double Point**	K	L

M	N	O
P	R	S
T	V **Double Point**	W **Double Point**
A	B	C

Name That Shape

Purpose

To have students play a game as a culminating activity on a unit about shapes.

To Make

Copy the game board from page 98 onto poster board as is or enlarge it to desired size. Color any six of the shapes black. Color the rest of the shapes different colors to make the game board more attractive. Laminate the game board.

Copy the game cards from pages 99–100 onto poster board. Laminate the cards and cut them out.

You will need two game pieces, one for each team. Use two different colored paper clips or two clothespins (use magic markers to paint one red and one blue).

⏰ Preparation time—45 minutes

To Play

Place the game cards face down. Divide the class into two teams, the red team and the blue team.

Ask a red team member to draw a card and give it to you. Read the question aloud. If the student answers the question correctly, he or she moves the team's marker to that shape. If the student answers incorrectly, the blue team has a chance to answer the question. If the marker lands on a black shape, that team loses a turn.

Have the teams take turns. The first team to reach the finish wins.

Books to Use

Circles by Mary Elizabeth Salzmann. ABDO Publishing Co., 2000. Pictures and text relate circles to the child's real world surroundings.

The Greedy Triangle by Marilyn Burns. Scholastic, 1994. A dissatisfied triangle samples life as other shapes.

Rectangles by Mary Elizabeth Salzmann. ABDO Publishing Co., 2000. Simple picture book of rectangles found in a child's everyday life.

Squares by Mary Elizabeth Salzmann. ABDO Publishing Co., 2000. Simple text describing squares is combined with pictures of squares found all around us.

Triangles by Mary Elizabeth Salzmann. ABDO Publishing Co., 2000. Simple text with real-life triangle pictures.

Name That Shape—Game Board

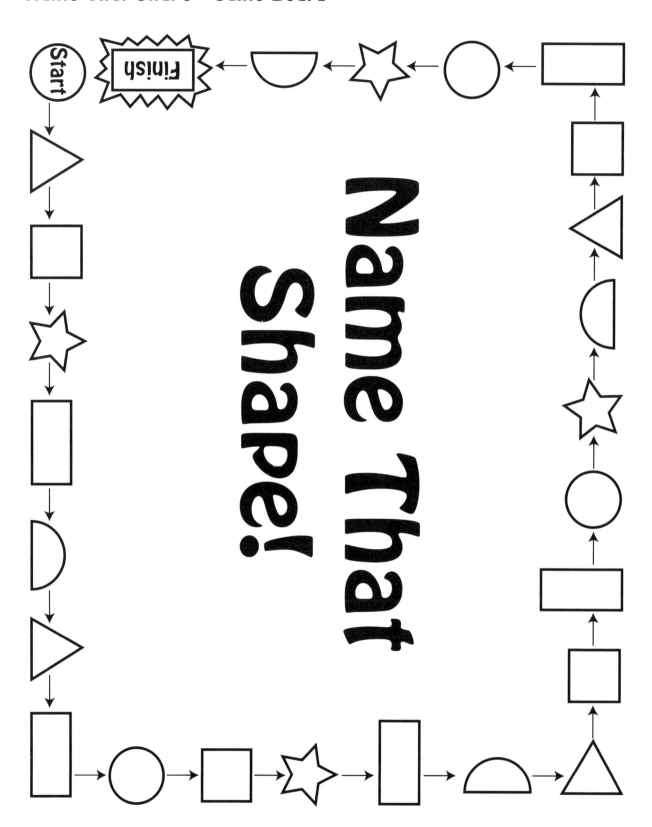

I have no straight lines.	You can see me twinkle in the night sky.	I only have three sides.	I am shaped like a door.
I have two long sides and two short sides.	A roof is often shaped like me.	A clock looks like me.	I have four corners, but not all of my sides are the same length.
I have four sides that are all the same length.	I am what you have if you cut a circle in half.	I am shaped like dice.	If you ate half of a pizza, the half that is left would look like me.
When you do good work, your teacher might put me on your paper.	I am round.	A refrigerator is shaped like me.	I have five points.
Your belly button is shaped like me.	I have three points.	Your teacher's desktop is shaped like me.	I have no points and no corners.

Name That Shape—Game Cards and Answers

Put two of me together just right, and you will make a circle.	The paper you write on is shaped like me.	I have a curved line and a straight line.	The sail of a sailboat is often shaped like me.
Cut me in half and I will make two semicircles.	The sun is shaped like me.	I am one side of a cube.	Most books are shaped like me.
Five triangles make up a whole of me.	I am shaped like a ruler.	I could roll down a hill.	Wheels on a car are shaped like me.

Answers:

Circle

I have no straight lines.

A clock looks like me.

I am round.

Your belly button is shaped like me.

I have no points and no corners.

Cut me in half and I will make two semicircles.

The sun is shaped like me.

I could roll down a hill.

Wheels on a car are shaped like me.

Semi-circle

I am what you have if you cut a circle in half.

If you ate half of a pizza, the half that is left would look like me.

Put two of me together just right, and you'll make a circle.

I have a curved line and a straight line.

Star

You can see me twinkle in the night sky.

When you do good work, your teacher might put me on your paper.

I have five points.

Five triangles make up a whole of me.

Triangle

I only have three sides.

A roof is often shaped like me.

I have three points.

The sail of a sailboat is often shaped like me.

Rectangle

I am shaped like a door.

I have two long sides and two short sides.

I have four corners, but not all of my sides are the same length.

A refrigerator is shaped like me.

Your teacher's desktop is shaped like me.

The paper you write on is shaped like me.

Most books are shaped like me.

I am shaped like a ruler.

Square

I have four sides that are all the same length.

I am shaped like dice.

I am one side of a cube.

Circle Sit

Purpose

To have students play a game as a culminating activity on a unit about shapes.

To Make

Prepare questions related to shapes or use the game card statements from Name that Shape on pages 99–100. Display the shapes that will be used: star, triangle, square, circle, semi-circle and rectangle.

⏰ Preparation time—10 minutes

To Play

Divide the class into two teams. Have each team stand in a circle. Ask a player on one team a question about shapes. If the answer is correct, the student sits down on the circle's edge. If the answer is incorrect, the student remains standing and the other team has a chance to answer the question. If they answer correctly, that player sits down on the circle's edge. The next question is directed to the team that answered the question correctly.

The game continues with the teams taking turns answering questions. The first team to have all its members sitting in a circle wins.

Grade Appropriate Skills Index

	K	1	2	3	4	5	6	Fiction	Nonfiction	Call Numbers	Biography	Geography	Social Studies	Science/Math	Pg.
RESOURCES OF THE MEDIA CENTER															
Chatter Books			✔	✔	✔	✔		✔	✔		✔				7
Word Play			✔	✔	✔	✔		✔	✔	✔	✔				9
4 x 4			✔	✔	✔	✔	✔	✔	✔	✔	✔				11
Lucky Numbers				✔	✔	✔	✔	✔	✔						14
Circle Book Toss		✔	✔	✔				✔	✔		✔				17
Biography Brainstorm			✔	✔	✔			✔	✔						20
CALL NUMBERS															
Small Steps, Giant Steps				✔	✔	✔	✔	✔	✔	✔	✔				23
Find That Book!				✔	✔	✔		✔	✔						26
FICTION BOOKS															
Cover Four		✔	✔					✔							28
Listen Carefully!			✔	✔	✔			✔							32
Wipeout!	✔	✔	✔					✔							33
Tic Tac Toe	✔	✔	✔					✔							35
Picture Detective	✔	✔	✔	✔				✔							38
Boards Up!	✔	✔	✔					✔							42
Write-On, Junie B.	✔	✔	✔					✔							44
Pickin' Time	✔	✔	✔					✔							55
Cover-Up	✔	✔	✔					✔							60
Caldecott Ping-Pong		✔	✔	✔				✔							66
Find Your Match		✔						✔		✔					68
What's in Katy's Pockets?	✔							✔							70
THEME GAMES															
Hopping Around Australia				✔	✔	✔		✔	✔			✔	✔	✔	77
Tangram Puzzle			✔	✔	✔			✔	✔			✔	✔		80
Reach the Poles			✔	✔	✔	✔		✔	✔			✔	✔	✔	84
A Story, A Story Game		✔	✔					✔	✔				✔		89
A—My Name Is Amazon				✔	✔	✔		✔	✔				✔	✔	93
Name That Shape	✔	✔	✔					✔	✔					✔	97
Circle Sit	✔	✔	✔					✔	✔					✔	101